MW01045089

Technology Pioneers

Jeff Bezos

Jennifer Strand

abdopublishing.com

Published by Abdo Zoom™, PO Box 398166, Minneapolis, Minnesota 55439. Copyright © 2017 by Abdo Consulting Group, Inc. International copyrights reserved in all countries. No part of this book may be reproduced in any form without written permission from the publisher. Abdo Zoom™ is a trademark and logo of Abdo Consulting Group, Inc.

Printed in the United States of America, North Mankato, Minnesota
092016
012017

Cover Photo: Reed Saxon/AP Images
Interior Photos: Reed Saxon/AP Images, 1; Ted S. Warren/AP Images, 4, 13; iStockphoto, 5, 6–7, 10, 15, 17; Seth Poppel/Yearbook Library, 7, 8; Maxiphoto/iStockphoto, 9; Barry Sweet/AP Images, 14; Mark Lennihan/AP Images, 16, 19; Ross D. Franklin/AP Images, 18

Editor: Brienna Rossiter
Series Designer: Madeline Berger
Art Direction: Dorothy Toth

Publisher's Cataloging-in-Publication Data
Names: Strand, Jennifer, author.
Title: Jeff Bezos / by Jennifer Strand.
Description: Minneapolis, MN : Abdo Zoom, 2017. | Series: Technology pioneers
    | Includes bibliographical references and index.
Identifiers: LCCN 2016948682 | ISBN 9781680799248 (lib. bdg.) |
    ISBN 9781624025105 (ebook) | 9781624025662 (Read-to-me ebook)
Subjects: LCSH: Bezos, Jeffrey, 1964- --Juvenile literature. | Amazon.com
    (Firm)--Juvenile literature. | Internet bookstores--United States--History--
    Juvenile literature. | Electronic commerce--United States--Biography--
    Juvenile literature. | Businessmen--United States--Biography--Juvenile
    literature. | Electronic books--History--Juvenile literature. | Kindle (Electronic
    book reader)--Juvenile literature.
Classification: DDC 381.4500/092 [B]--dc23
LC record available at http://lccn.loc.gov/2016948682

Table of Contents

Introduction

Jeff Bezos is an American **entrepreneur.**

He founded Amazon.com.
It is a shopping website.

Early Life

Jeff was born on January 12, 1964.
He grew up in Texas.

He worked on
his grandfather's ranch.

Jeff liked to build things.

His school had a computer.
He often stayed after school
to work on it.

The Internet was becoming **popular**.

Bezos studied computers in college. Then he got a job in New York. He worked in **finance**.

Bezos started an online store. He called the store Amazon. It sold books. Its website launched on July 16, 1995.

13

Amazon.com was easy to use. The prices were cheap, too. Soon it was very popular.

It began to sell many things besides books.

In 2007 Amazon
created the Kindle.

It was a small device. But it could store thousands of e-books.

Legacy

Bezos is an **innovator**.
Amazon changed how
people buy things.

It is known for its fast delivery.
Plus Bezos continues to
add new features.

Jeff Bezos

Born: January 12, 1964

Birthplace: Albuquerque, New Mexico

Wife: MacKenzie Tuttle

Known For: Bezos is an entrepreneur. He created the shopping website Amazon.com.

Key Dates

1964: Jeffrey Preston Jorgensen is born on January 12.

1968: Jeff's mother remarries. He takes the last name Bezos.

1994: Bezos moves to Seattle, Washington, to start Amazon.com.

1995: Amazon.com launches on July 16.

2007: Amazon announces the Kindle e-reader.

2013: Bezos buys the *Washington Post* newspaper.

Glossary

entrepreneur - a person who starts a business or businesses.

finance - the way businesses, banks, and governments use and manage their money.

innovator - someone who does something in a new way.

popular - liked or enjoyed by many people.

ranch - a big farm where animals are raised.

Booklinks

For more information
on **Jeff Bezos**, please visit
booklinks.abdopublishing.com

Zoom In on Biographies!

Learn even more with the Abdo Zoom
Biographies database. Check out
abdozoom.com for more information.

Index